SO MANY YEARS

A Juneteenth Story

Words by Anne Wynter   Pictures by Jerome Pumphrey

Clarion Books
An Imprint of HarperCollinsPubishers

Clarion Books is an imprint of HarperCollins Publishers.

So Many Years
Text copyright © 2025 by Anne Wynter
Illustrations copyright © 2025 by Jerome Pumphrey
All rights reserved. Manufactured in Capriate San Gervasio, Italy.
No part of this book may be used or reproduced in any manner whatsoever
without written permission except in the case of brief quotations embodied
in critical articles and reviews. For information address HarperCollins
Children's Books, a division of HarperCollins Publishers,
195 Broadway, New York, NY 10007.
www.harpercollinschildrens.com

ISBN 978-0-06-308114-7

The artist used acrylic paint on hardboard panels and Photoshop to create
the illustrations for this book.
Typography by Dana Fritts
25 26 27 28 29 RTLO 10 9 8 7 6 5 4 3 2 1
First Edition

How would you dress
after so many years
of mending your clothes with rags?

How would you sing
after so many years
of writing your songs in code?

How would you eat
after so many years
of making your meals from scraps?

How would you dance
after so many years
of working through waves of pain?

After so many years
that were stolen

again

and again

and again . . .

. . . oh, how you would dress!

LIFT EVERY VOICE AND SING

JUNETEENTH 1950

Oh, how you would sing!

Oh, how you would eat!

Oh, how you would dance!

Oh, how you would celebrate . . .

. . . so many years . . .

of a life . . .

. . . fully yours . . .

. . . fully free.

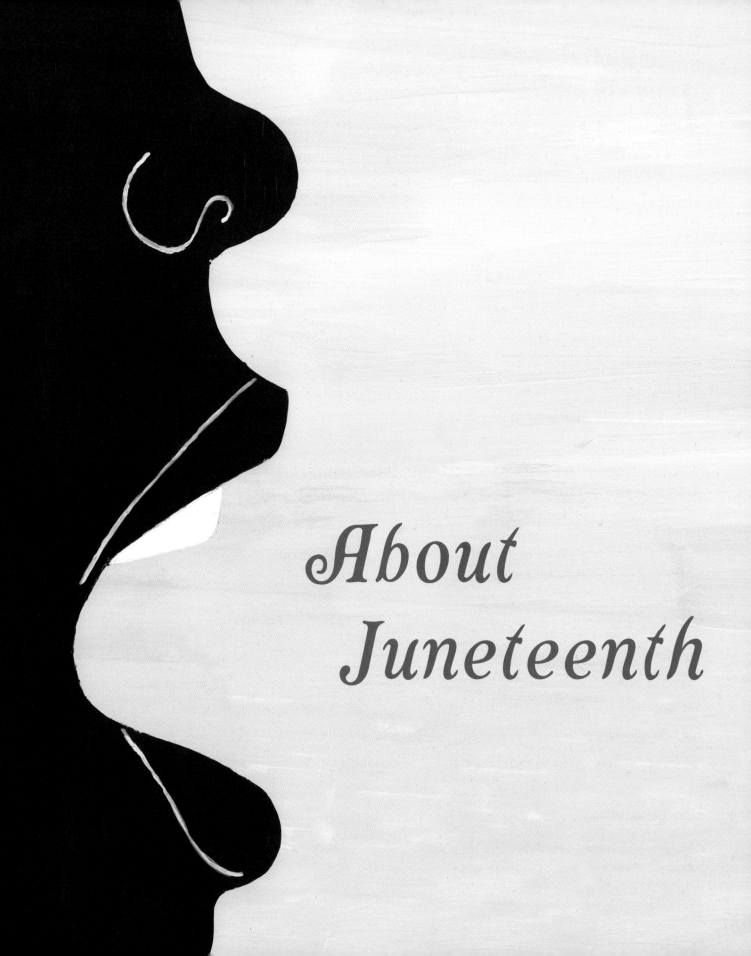

About
Juneteenth

In the 1860s, close to one third of Texans were enslaved Black people. Enslaved people were not only forced to work for free, but most of them had no choice over where they lived, how they spent their days, whether they could remain with their families, or what their futures would look like.

For many enslaved Texans, life changed on June 19, 1865.* On the date that would become known as Juneteenth (a combination of the words "June" and "nineteenth"), Union Major General Gordon Granger stood on the balcony of Ashton Villa in Galveston, Texas, and announced that all enslaved people were now free.

General Granger's announcement ended slavery for many people—but not for everyone. Some Black Texans were still forced to provide free labor for months or even years, while others were met with violence when they tried to leave their enslavers. Even for those who could leave, life as a formerly enslaved Black person wasn't easy or fair. In the decades since slavery ended, laws and practices like the Black codes, Jim Crow, redlining, and mass incarceration have extended the cruel legacy of slavery.

In spite of the many challenges ahead, General Granger's June 19, 1865 announcement was a major step forward in the march toward equality. Since then, June 19 has been a day of remembrance and jubilation. Over the decades, Texans have commemorated Juneteenth with festivals, pageants, parades, dances, sporting events, concerts, worship services, speeches, and more.

Popular activities include reading the Emancipation Proclamation, singing "Lift Every Voice and Sing," and enjoying large feasts with foods like barbecue, greens, potato salad, cakes, pies, and red soda water. Celebrations range in size from small backyard picnics to multiday festivals that draw tens of thousands of attendees.

In 1979, state representative Al Edwards sponsored a bill that would make Juneteenth an official Texas holiday beginning in 1980. While Juneteenth started out as a Texas celebration, it quickly spread to other states and, eventually, to other countries. In 2021, Juneteenth finally became a national holiday.

You can continue the tradition of Juneteenth—also known as Emancipation Day or Freedom Day—by finding an event in your community or by gathering with your loved ones to remember the millions of enslaved people and to celebrate this day of jubilation and freedom.

----

* This came more than two years after Abraham Lincoln issued the Emancipation Proclamation on January 1, 1863, which declared that enslaved people in rebelling states would be free—if the Union won the war. It took a long time for the news of the Confederate surrender to reach Texas, a Confederate stronghold. The Emancipation Proclamation, the end of the Civil War, Juneteenth, and the ratification of the Thirteenth, Fourteenth, and Fifteenth Amendments were all important steps on the long path to Black people's freedom and equality.

Lift Every Voice and Sing

Words by **James Weldon Johnson**
Music by **John Rosamond Johnson**

Lift ev'ry voice and sing,
Till earth and heaven ring,
Ring with the harmonies of Liberty;
Let our rejoicing rise
High as the list'ning skies,
Let it resound loud as the rolling sea.
Sing a song full of the faith that the dark past has taught us
Sing a song full of the hope that the present has brought us;
Facing the rising sun of our new day begun,
Let us march on till victory is won.

Stony the road we trod,
Bitter the chast'ning rod
Felt in the days when hope unborn had died;
Yet with a steady beat,
Have not our weary feet
Come to the place for which our fathers sighed?
We have come over a way that with tears has been watered.
We have come, treading our path thro' the blood of the slaughtered,
Out from the gloomy past,
Till now we stand at last
Where the white gleam of our bright star is cast.

God of our weary years,
God of our silent tears,
Thou who hast brought us thus far on the way;
Thou who hast by Thy might,
Led us into the light,
Keep us forever in the path, we pray,
Lest our feet stray from the places, our God, where we met Thee;
Lest our hearts, drunk with the wine of the world, we forget Thee;
Shadowed beneath Thy hand,
May we forever stand,
True to our God, true to our Native land.